Kids Rule!

Let the Message Run Free

Poetry by 7-11 year-olds

Edited by
Annabel Cook

First published in Great Britain in 2007 by:
Young Writers
Remus House
Coltsfoot Drive
Peterborough
PE2 9JX
Telephone: 01733 890066
Website: www.youngwriters.co.uk
All Rights Reserved
© Copyright Contributors 2007
SB ISBN 978-1 84431 194 1

Foreword

'Kids Rule!' poetry competition inspired children from all over the UK to put pen to paper and imagine themselves in the position of being in charge of the country. With enthusiasm and energy they have expressed the many things they would change to make our world a better place.

We are therefore pleased to present *'Kid Rule! Let The Message Run Free'*. Having received such a large amount of entries, we hope you'll agree the poems selected are both enlightening and enjoyable. They will entertain and give pause for thought.

Young Writers was established in 1991 to promote poetry and creative writing to school children and encourage them to read, write and enjoy it. Here at Young Writers we are sure you'll agree that this unique edition achieves our aim and celebrates today's wealth of young writing talent. We hope you and your family continue to enjoy *'Kids Rule! Let The Message Run Free'* for many years to come.

Contents

The Poems

Prize may differ from products shown

Congratulations Zoe!

We loved your alphabet poem.
You have won a fab Mp3 player!
Well done!

Alphabet Orders

If I ran the country
I would be,
Kind and caring
Now let's see . . .

A world full of fun, with roller coasters and rides
B right smiles on every face, to which everyone must abide
C reativity and exploration, to free your mind
    And build your self-esteem
D ancing and singing, to let your light beam
E nthusiasm in all we do, truth and faith and hope all around
F riends for everyone, mates stick together and stand their ground
G ratefulness and fairness, so that no one is left out
H appiness spread across the world, no wars, no fights
    No hideousness to be heard about
I nside we must think before we act, dream don't worry
    And you will reach your goal
J ustice to the environment, to do this we must all play a role
K indness to be shared out, this way we all feel equal
L ively and healthy is the never-ending sequel
M oney, not poverty, is the life to live
N eat and tidy countries, that all share and give
O verwhelm your family, to become like a tightly woven mesh
P eople to think deeper about others, not just to see them
I n the flesh
Q uestions and answers are not left to be undiscovered
R ainbows, not rain, colours all around, the sky would be smothered
S wearing to be banned, no bad language to be heard
T reats every day, your sweets have been lured
U ltimate challenges, but everyone will succeed
V ariable fairness, this is what the world needs
W onderful plants and animals, a joy to watch, they're not a threat
X ylophones are more popular, this challenge has got to be met
Y ears to go by quicker, so that they're not a bore
Z oe is the Pime Minister . . . do you need to hear more?

Zoe Hyde (11)

Kids Rule

If I ruled the country
Children would drive
And even be allowed
To shop and buy

If I ruled the country
I would stop all wars
Find the cure for cancer
And rearrange the laws

If I ruled the country
Kids would teach the teachers
As well as teachers teaching them
Plus all school uniform would be banned

If I ruled the country
Parents would pay their children
And poverty would end
Children would eat whatever they wanted
And drive you round the bend

But, of course we know
That this will never happen
So keep on dreaming!

Audrey Borquaye (10)

The Kiddie Kids Rule

I'm the kid who rules the world,
I want to tell my rules of excellence

Chocolate and crisps, we all love it
I'm so sorry, it's no longer on meals,
The best choice is to have fruit or vegetables
I strongly agree with that deal

No more homework when we come back from school
Tell the teachers that's the rule,
Teachers wear uniforms, kids wear what they like
Take the teachers cars and make them use their bikes

Extra Christmas holidays to play with our toys
Teachers must give money to the girls and boys,
We deliver pizzas whenever we like
No more fighting, no more wars

Everyone must do their very best
To make this world a better place,
I want to finally say two things:
Eat your five a day, that's the best way
Plus, plus, plus, keep the environment clean *every day!*

Charlotte Gough (11)

If I Were Prime Minister

If I were Prime Minister
I would give away, at least one treat a day
To those who really need it
I would show my love to the world
And help stop the pollution.

I would build more playgrounds
With swings and slides
To play and mess about in
And hang out with your friends.

I would show 'The Simpsons' four hours a day
Then take a walk along the beach
To see what kind of creatures I could see
Dolphins, sharks and whales as well.

I would let everyone see the sights
Of my brand new funfair
With roller coasters and waterslides
With bumper cars and a Ferris wheel
That go round and round till the world spins.

Out of all the things I would do as prime minister
I would not create wars, but create peace!

Lauren Stokes (12)

Kids Rule!

If I were Prime Minister,
Then homework would be banned,
If anyone protested,
I'd let them have their say,
Then lock them up and walk away,
Every street would have a park,
So kids could play all day.

Elliot Robert McMenemy (12)

Vote For Me

If I ruled the country
This is what I'd do
I'd get everyone together
To have fun with you

I'd work hard for my country
I'd work hard for myself
I'd work hard for my family
And I'd work hard for everyone else

I'd give the children whatever they wanted
I'd give the adults money
I'd give the grandparents lovely lives
And they'd be bright and sunny

I'd give you a fabulous life
So no one could complain
I'm the best Prime Minister
I'm not to blame

Vote for me
It would be fair
But not for Tony Blair.

Gledisa Musollari (9)

If I'd Got To Run The Country For A Day, There Would Be A Few Changes . . .

All children would be in charge,
Adults would be made to go to bed wearing nappies
At 8.00pm sharp;
There would be theme parks in everybody's
Back gardens that never close,
A clothes allowance of £100 every day (paid by parents)
And every child could make their own allowance
That the parents had to pay!

Oh, how I would love to be Prime Minister
For just one day!

Jhon Bateman (10)

Why Can't Kids Rule?

Why can't kids rule?
Have no books and have no school,
Eating sweet things, chocolates, cakes,
Can't you adults give us a break?

Pocket money rises,
Are really no surprises,
'Cause they are only a pound or two,
If you ask me,
They really should be
A rise that is really cool.

If you still don't get it,
You're going to regret it,
We are better than *you!*

Surabhi Desai (11)

Kids Rule!

If I were Prime Minister,
I'd be as hard as steel,
To the moaning grown-ups,
Because they beg like a seal!

I'd make an announcement
And then I'd declare,
A list of changes,
That were extremely fair.

And every day at school,
You could cook, write or paint
And that I shall be hopefully known,
As Emma, the Patron Saint.

Now here I come,
To the annoying part,
I'm sorry to all nice adults
And yes, I do have a heart.

Now, therefore,
I would be in charge,
I'd ship all adults to France,
On every single barge.

For girls, I'd make a special shop,
Called 'Beauti-Licious Boutique'
And for the boys, I'd make a different shop,
That's let's say, is unique.

In every meal that is eaten,
There must be at least ten chocolate bars
And I would like to ask if you could recycle,
Or you will get a large fine (but smaller than Mars).

I'd hope my people would like me
And treat me with respect,
But to be honest with myself,
That's a lot of things to expect!

Emma Pike (11)

My Rules

It's compulsory to eat ice cream,
It's one of your five a day,
And when you do homework,
The teacher has to pay!

Sprouts are a no-no,
So is maths and RE,
School is only on Mondays,
And chocolate bars are free!

Parents must give out sweets,
At least every weekend,
And give their children lots and lots,
Of pocket money to spend!

No more bullying,
Give money to the poor,
Recycle cardboard, paper,
Plastic and much, much more!

Don't forget to eat,
Some fruit and veg each day,
Be kind to each other,
This is all I say!

Claudia Graham (11)

New Rules In Town

The first thing I'd do
Is scare the teachers
By shouting, *'Boo!'*
I'd ban all school
Make the teachers cool
Hmm then what should I do?
Aha! Eat chocolate and chips
With no dips
And they are the new rules in town!

Markieta Venter (9)

Kids In Charge

Everlasting chocolate
And essays thrown to dust,
Nothing in the dictionary,
Why?
Cos I'm in charge.

Homework's a no-no,
But sweeties are good
And there's everlasting peace in the world,
Why?
Cos I'm in charge.

Holidays last forever
And TVs are in every room,
Ice cream sundaes are on demand,
Why?
Cos I'm in charge.

Kids will be in charge forever,
Of that of which I am sure,
For we know where to toe the line,
But adults aren't so sure.

Charlotte Self (11)

Kids Rule!

Us kids are the best people to rule the world
Every girls' hair could be curled
No school, *no* bedtime
Then at least we can be cool
That's why kids should rule.
Maybe not pay anything to get sweets and stuff
Watch the footie in big stadiums
Get to meet the players and stuff
All our food should be chips, chips and more chips
Go on holiday to Las Vegas and even more
Are those enough reasons why us kids should rule the world?
Can I have money?
My mum gives me one, but Dad gives me five
Oh well, we can live, can you?
You see, if kids ruled, maybe we'd stop asking for this and that
It doesn't matter anyway, cos we are the kids who are going to
Rule the world!

Kayleigh Thomas (10)

Kids Rule

If I were Tony Blair and had a country to run,
The land would be fair and much more fun.

Swearing in public would not be wise
And having good manners would be strongly advised.

Keep troublesome dogs on leashes and leads
And clean up their mess as well, if you please!

Public transport is the way to go,
We could save the planet, you know.

Homework in primary school is very bad,
It's OK in secondary, but for my age, it's sad!

All of these things may seem very remote,
But if I were Prime Minister, would I get your vote?

Harriet Dagnall (10)

Kids Rule!

Kids rule, they are so cool
But they all hate school
So, if I could change the rules
Parents would go to school

Kids would get £10 a day
And do nothing but play
They would not have to eat veg
And there would be no set time for bed!

We would all have to be nice to each other
And love and respect our mother
We would have chips for lunch and tea
And everyone would have to listen to me!

We would watch as much TV as we liked
And homework would take a hike
We wouldn't read books
But at comics we would take a look

Kids rule because they are cool
But we all know we need school!
I will always listen to what my mum and dad have to say
Because tomorrow is another day!

Hayden Stevens (10)

Untitled

Homework is thrown away,
Children never have to pay,
Oh, did I mention that,
Everyone has wings like bats?
School is only for one day,
But you can still scream, shout and play,
Wishes are free to roam
And that's the end of the poem.

Iona Macrae (9)

Kids Rule

When kids rule, there's no school,
It's chocolate morning, noon and night
And if you think that would give your parents a fright,
Then it's video games all day long,
Even though we know it's wrong,
Homework is banished, the law is passed,
Time for some fun, at long last.

It doesn't have to be like this,
We are not always so selfish,
We help people, young and old
And sometimes do what we are told,
I would spend my money with lots of care,
To make sure there's food for all to share,
I'd protect the Earth, it's our only home
And make sure that children are not left alone,
If I were PM, this is what I would do,
You can vote me in, it's up to you!

Sam Felton (9)

You Forgot Something Mr Blair

Cough! Cough! Cough!
The old man splutters,
I'd ban smoking,
To give him a life.

Cry! Cry! Cry!
The baby cries of starvation,
I'd raise money,
To give her a life.

Brum! Brum! Brum!
The cars omit pollution,
I'd bring in more bicycles,
To give us a life.

Groan! Groan! Groan!
The old woman groans,
I'd extend the NHS,
Or she won't have a life.

Oh no! Oh no! Oh no!
Exclaimed the Year 6 boy,
I'd bring in more teachers,
Or he won't have a life.

Bang! Bang! Bang!
Off goes a bomb,
I'd bring in more security,
Or we all won't be alive.

Jack Wagman (10)

If I Were Prime Minister

If I were Prime Minister
I would give pocket money every day
With half going to the poor
Everyone will have a home
So there is no one left on the street

If I were Prime Minister
I would give chocolate and sweets for breakfast
Cake and chips for lunch
Doughnuts and cookies for dinner
And fizzy drinks whenever you want

If I were Prime Minister
Parents would not tell us what to do
Or nag us to do our homework
They wouldn't tell us to go to bed
But let us do what we want

If I were Prime Minister
The world would be a better place.

Emma Lee (10)

Being Prime Minister

Being prime minister,
I would not let any child
Go to bed early.

Less sleep,
More fun in the day!

Being prime minister,
I would make homework
A non-existent word.

Less work,
More fun at the weekend!

Being prime minister,
I would let everyone
Go on holiday for free.

Less schoolwork,
More sunshine!

Tamara Press (10)

Give Me A Call . . .

Chocolates for free,
Chips for tea.
No need for school uniform,
Or veg or corn.

No school,
Every house must have a pool.
£1,000,000 pocket money,
You should be happy because I'm not being funny.

No one shall ever die,
It would be hard, but it is no lie.
Red roses for sale,
Only 10 pence for a female.

More candy and sweets,
No more cheese that stinks of feet.
Later bed times for all,
You can't possibly get bored,
But if you do give me a call!

Abby Posner (10)

Prime Minister

When I am Prime Minister and ruler of the country

I would make lots of changes to the country
Like parents not going to work every weekday
And it becoming compulsory to have fun every day.

Extending school holidays and banning school uniform
And perhaps I would abolish homework and tests too!
TVs in every classroom, all channels you could want
A selection of chocolates and sweeties would upset healthy eating.

When people go shopping to town or locally,
The wouldn't need purses, as everything would be free.

If I became Prime Minister
As you can see
Everyone would be happy
But it would be unforeseen.

Grace Davis (9)

Vote Rosie!

If I were the president . . .

There would be chocolate for every meal,
Parents *have* to pay £50 pocket money a day,
The adults do all the work
And kids just sit around all day.

If I were the president . . .

Life would be a wonderland,
Going to the seaside,
Playing in the sand.

Rosie Haftel (10)

Kids

K ids will not go to school
They'll stay home and play ball
I f you disobey our rule
You will have no faith at all
D o as we say, don't be a fool
You must remember kids are cool
S o, parents respect kids now rule
It's time for you to go back to school!

Robin Bernard (7)

If I Were Prime Minister

If I were Prime Minister
I would run the country right
I would make the days much longer
And keep schoolwork out of sight
We would eat chocolate all day
In-between having fun
Our country would be safe
Because by me it would be run!

Jack Davis (10)

Untitled

Teachers will teach,
Workers will work,
Sellers will sell
And I will just smirk.

Give money to poor,
Keep yourself safe,
Remember to be healthy
And always behave.

Listen to what I tell you,
Even though you might not like it,
But you all chose me yourselves,
So this is how you'll have it!

Daniel Liubarski (10)

When I'm Prime Minister

When I'm Prime Minister
Everyone will play football at least once a week
The Spurs badge will be everywhere
And you can arrange to see football players
Also football kits will be free!

When I'm Prime Minister
Kids eat what they want
Even if it's sweets every day
All vegetables will be thrown away
And you eat what you like.

When I'm Prime Minister
You can drive at 10+
Or leave school whenever
And there will be no age limits
At cinemas.

When I'm Prime Minister
You won't learn maths or science
You learn about computer games
And you watch TV
And school lunches will be nice.

So remember
Play football once a week
Throw vegetables away
Don't bother saying age limits
Make school fun
But most of all
Respect your youngsters!

Alex Woffenden (10)

When I Am President!

When I am president, there will be no wars,
When I am president, there will be no laws,
When I am president, there will be no lies,
When I am president, people must eat pies!

When I am president, people must be kind,
For if they are not, they will just be fined!
And if people fight,
Then their future won't be bright!

When I am president, people will not disobey me
And if they do, then they will be thrown out to sea.
When I am president, no one will be scared,
When I am president, money will be shared.

Anyway, it's not like I'll get chosen
To be President!

Jake Levison (10)

Kids Rule

If I were Prime Minister, I would destroy all homework
If I were Prime Minister, I would make sweets every meal
If I were Prime Minister, I would make there be no school
If I were Prime Minister, I would make Big Ben a chocolate fountain
If I were Prime Minister, I would make grown-ups, children's slaves
If I were Prime Minister, I would make peace
If I were Prime Minister, I would make there be no bad people!

Olive Pierre Cobrin (9)

If I Were The Prime Minister!

If I were the prime minister,
I would change the rules,
All the kids would have fun
And all the parents would be fools.

If I were the prime minister,
I would make world peace,
Everyone would be happy
And have a big feast.

If I were the prime minister,
Homework would be gone,
All the kids would be free,
But school would still be on.

If I were the prime minister,
Kids won't have to eat fruit
And no vegetables either,
So don't ever toot!

Amy Phillips (10)

A Chocolate World

When I am Prime Minister,
I will make the whole world into chocolate,
Prison won't seem so sinister,
With bars made of chocolate logs.

People would taste so yummy,
They'd eat their arms and legs,
Watch out for your friends,
You'll end up in their tummy.

Maltesers for eyes,
A lolly for a nose,
I would love to eat my brother,
If he was one of those.

I would make it rain chocolate milk,
Snow fruit flakes,
Thunder crackling candy
And hail gobstoppers.

The world will be a sweet place
With me in charge!

Hannah Wagman (8)

Kids Rules

If I were Prime Minister
I would say:
No homework
You don't have to behave all day!

If I were Prime Minister
This is what I would say:
You will get to play
Every single day!

If I were Prime Minister
I would say:
You can have ice cream, I say
You can have ice cream every day!

Devon Shoob (7)

Invasion

G reat, the best . . . who are we?
R uled by grown-ups utterly.
O ften we're crying and thinking we're dying,
W e're the children. We will plan an escape, cheating and lying . . .
N o need! Now I'm Prime Minister, it's children galore,

U p with many a new law!
P ocket money for parents will be 2p a month, is that clear?
S trictly no arguing, or it will be 2p a year . . .

W orld wide web entirely forbidden to those over twenty,
A t least £500 pocket money every week per child should be plenty.
T he parents must go to bed at 7pm - that's right!
C hildren, however, can party all night.

H omework abolished for children but compulsory to teachers every day,
O nly grown-ups washing up, while we sit down and play.
U ntidy bedrooms allowed, fizzy drinks spilt and gum stuck everywhere.
T hose are my laws, so goodbye Tony Blair!

Nathan Sharp (7)

My Kids Rule Poem

Make all health foods
For poor people to eat
A price that is cheaper
Than any other treats.

What fun it would be
To have one piece
Of homework a week
Late nights for all of the kids.

The sports events made cheaper
For all kids to see
No more than £5
I think is a good fee.

Ethan Gold (7)

Becoming Prime Minister

'Me' becoming Prime Minister!
A change of prime minister
In demand
Yes, a new prime minister
In command.

I would build in every school
Air conditioned cinemas to keep you entertained and cool
Or better yet, a mini chocolate and sweet factory,
To recharge children's energy battery.

I would make teachers sit in detention
To have a feel of what it is to be in urinary retention
Free holidays for every child to Disneyland
Fulfilling their dreams of becoming Thumbelina or Peter Pan.

Kids I wish could rule someday
To become Prime Minister I hope and pray
This job I imagine to be fun
For a kid to be giving adults the ultimatum
I guess it won't be easy for a kid in this world today
But a change of prime minister is not far away.

Daneille Murdock (11)

Victory Speech

I'm Prime Minister, hiya everyone!
First I'd like to have some fun.
Anyone eating vegetables will be kicked out of the country,
Eat chips, pizza and anything munchy.
Now I'd like to talk about schools,
They're all going to be shut down,
If any parent takes their kid,
The parent is going to be turned into a clown.
There will be lots of other rules
But I'm getting a bit bored,
So come back tomorrow
To hear much, much more!

Chloe Lindridge (9)

If I Were The PM . . .

If I ran the country
Then here's what I'd do -

I'd ban homework and stealing
And mean teachers too

I'd bring back Robin Hood
To do what he did best,
Rob the rich and share with the poor

And Florence Nightingale
To look after the sick and infirm

I'd ask a scientist to invent a rocket bus
To take people on trips to the moon

I'd make a better job, I am sure
And the world would be a happier place to be.

Katy Langley (11)

If I Were . . .

If I were Prime Minister
I would make sure
Kids told parents what to do
Homework would be abolished
Kids would have presents every day.

For tea we would have
Chips, nuggets and baked potato
We would eat anything between meals
We would love it
Along with our 6ft chocolate fountain
We would do whatever we wanted, because

Kids rule!

Lisa Berry (10)

If I Could Rule

If I could rule
And kids could drool
I would be as happy as can be
If I could rule
And if I could drool
Then I would be famous
I would like to solve mysteries
As well as rule
I would make people be nice to each other
As well as share
I would make the country a nice place
And everyone would have enough money.

Molly Brodie (8)

Kids Rule

Vote for me
And you will see,
That I will be,
The *best* prime minister ever!

I will make a resort land
And expand the greenhouse lands.

I will let you do and eat
Whatever you want to
Except letting anyone harm you.

I will give you a fund raise
And then people will give you praise.

Vote for me
And you will see,
That I will be,
The *best* prime minister ever!

I will help all the poor
And then pay them more.

I will abolish all the homework,
Then there will be no schoolwork.

I will stop all the wars
And then take people on tours
Around London.

Vote for me
And you will see,
That I will be,
The *best* prime minister ever!

I will watch TV all day
And lock the criminals away.

I will make people laugh
And give them half
Of my money.

I will bring back Cinderella,
Then put her back in the cellar!

Vote for me
And you will see,
That I will be,
The *best* prime minister ever!

Sarah Jinodu (11)

If I Were In Charge

If I were in charge, I would rule the world
It would always be summer, it would never be cold
I would bask in the sun all day, every day
No teachers to teach us, hip, hip, hooray
Now as for the sky, it would be a bright pink
Don't use your brain we have robots to think
Every meal would be chocolate galore
Because the law says, it's not bad anymore
My house will be ten times bigger and very large
Do what I say because I am in charge!

Bryony Challoner (11)

If

If kids ruled the country
I'd make people nicer to people
If we were so kind
No one would mind
We would care and share
Everywhere

If kids ruled the country
We would stop wars
All the sorrows
They have caused

If kids ruled the country
We would stop some laws
To help children through
Their parents' divorce.

Courtney Dunstan (11)

Kids Rule!

If I were Prime Minister,
I'd get rid of my sister,

If I ruled the country, here and now,
I'd buy a farm and own a cow,

If I ruled the country, day and night,
I'd herd the villains and give them a *fright!*

If I were Prime Minister and saw Tony Blair,
I'd turn around and say, 'Where's your hair?'

If I were Prime Minister, I'd buy a school,
Sack all the teachers and *let kids rule!*

Sean Brown (9)

Respect

R   ecycle more to save the world
E   veryone should be grateful for all the good
S   peed kills so respect the rules
P   lease be kind to each other
E   nvironment should be cared for
C   areful of what you have
T   he world would be better if we all showed respect.

Natasha Ward (7)

I'm The Prime Minister

I'm the prime minister, you do what you are told
I'm the prime minister and I am very bold
I'm the prime minister and every child must get £50 pocket money
I'm sure your parents won't think that's very funny
Chips all day
Until May
Then we all must eat hay!
Everyone must donate money to the poor
So they are not poor anymore
I'm the prime minister and this is my poem
Put your hands in your pocket and let's get going!

Katie Blennerhassett (10)

Kids Rule

One hundred pounds I would say
For pocket money every day
No science, English, maths or SATs
No homework and I am sure of that
The mums and dads work extra hard
To keep us off the fat and lard
I'm writing to you here and now
And next, I'm going to take a bow!

Angelica Lydia Cooke (10)

The Prime Minister

If I were the prime minister
Kids would rule the school!
If I were the prime minister
Teachers would be cool!

If I were head of parliament
Children would be bad
If I were head of parliament
Parents would go mad!

If I were the prime minister
I would feel the power
If I were the prime minister
There'd be junk food every hour!

Rebecca Downs (10)

Kids Rule!

If I ran the country, I would
Make people happy, for someone should
Everyone would have their own rights
So that we could stop all the fights
The environment would be a disaster
If we don't try to help it faster

Bullying should stop in school
So that it would be more cool
I want to help the world be fit
Everyone could do their bit
I would make sure
That no people were poor
If nobody was filled with sadness
Everyone could be overflowing with gladness

No fighting, meanness or killing
But the people must be willing

The world will be a better place
When everyone has a smile on their face.

Miriam Thompson (10)

If I Could Run The Country

If I could run the country
This is what I'd do;
I'd close the school immediately
To open up a zoo!

There'd be no end of money,
Gold and silver too,
There'd be mountain loads of chocolate
Enough for me and you.

Parents wouldn't need to work
They'd play with us all day,
They would obey our every rule
And do all that we say!

There would be shelf loads of books
That we'd read when we pleased,
We won't eat any manky foods
Especially Stilton cheese!

So vote me for Prime Minister
Don't leave your vote too late
My changes to the country
Will make our lives just great!

Gemma Hagon (10)

If I Were The Prime Minister For The Day . . .

If I were the prime minister for the day
I would make all homework go away!
I would make everything free!
And wouldn't chop down one more tree!
I would make sure that everyone had a home
And everything that we would need!
And I would make sure we lived in luxury!
Together we would save the world!
We would all eat ice cream that is swirled
I would recycle and cut down on rubbish
I would stop everyone being sluggish!
We would all be fair,
And we would all care,
If I were the prime minister for a day
All bad things would go away!

Niamh Collins (10)

If I Were To Run The Country!

If I were to run the country,
I would protect the environment,
By making sure rubbish would not be dropped
And would not pollute the world so much.

We would help the poor more,
To give them more money
And help them live a happy life.

For teachers to give us
A bit less homework.

If I were to run the country
It would change for the better!

Amy Horner (9)

That's Just How I Want It To Be!

I would make parents run bare down the street!
No one would make me eat meat
Vegetables would be a stranger to me!
And that's just how I want it to be!
Oh and how much money I would get
I just counted, but I always forget!
There would never be homework or school forever
And that's just how I want it to be
You would only have chocolate at each meal!
Cuts and bruises would soon heal
Our room would always get messy
But parents would deal with that
And that's just how I want it to be!
And that's just how I want it to be!

Abigail Martin (9)

If I Were . . .

If I were a ruler
I would not say I was cooler
I would say I'm normal
Just like you.

If I were like a queen
I would not be mean
I would make sure
Our town was clean.

These words are true
I'd say I was just like you!

Megan Louise Swift (8)

If I Ran The Country!

If I could tell people what to do,
I'd demand more pocket money
And chocolate too!

I'd have a pink mansion
With pink everywhere,
I'd also help the poor
To show I care!

I'd abolish homework
Forever and ever,
The teachers would be dumb
And the children really clever!

We'd protect the environment
And be kind to each other,
Even if you don't like
Your sister or brother.

I'd love a camera crew
To stand outside my double doors,
I'd definitely stop
All the ridiculous wars.

You know what I'd do
If I had my way,
I might even become
Prime Minister one day!

Georgina Dance (11)

Kids Rule!

If kids ruled the country
How would it be?
Ice cream and chocolate
For your lunch and your tea!
Say goodbye to teachers
Homework and all
Kids would graffiti
All over the wall!
It would be fun
It would be cool
But what would *you* do
If you had to rule?

Emily Hastings (10)

Untitled

If I were to run the country
I would replace weapons with sweets
And homework with chocolate
If I were to run the country
I would turn schools into water parks
And I would let kids have
Whatever they want for dinner
And the world would be made for kids.

Reshmi Ladwa (9)

Kids Rule!

In future, kids will rule
No chores to do at all
Kids could change the world
Kids could be the best
We could rule the street
And eat loads of sweets
Do what we want
Do what we feel
Kids could rule
Every school!

Toyanne Nelson Thomas (10)

Country Rules!

P arents *have* to serve all children
A lways get everything we want
R ight or wrong we get the best
E very day is a holiday
N ever go to school
T he best comes to those that don't wait
S weets we can have!

Amber Hopgood (8)

My Rules

If I were the boss, this is what I would do
I'd lock the teachers in the zoo,
I'd lock them in a monkey cage
And watch them shout and squirm with rage.
I'd throw them a banana and some nuts
And tell them, 'Stay! no ifs or buts'.
In the next cage goes Mom and Dad
Then my brother, who's really sad.

My rules are simple
But please be aware
They are nothing like the rules of Mr Blair.
Education out and TV in
Homework books go in the bin.
Veg is bad and sweets are good
And everyone's clothes should be covered in mud!

These are my rules
I am no yob
Vote for me
And give me the job!

Savannah Melville (9)

Country Runner

I would make everyone be kinder to others
I would run the country with respect
And have no one cut down the trees
Unless I give permission.
I would share with the poor
If they really need money
And the environment will be safer than before.
I will put an end to pollution
Cut down on tax fees
Reduce swimming pool costs to 50p
Stop all non-disabled parkers
Parking in disabled spaces.
Make a difference to the world
The hospitals need to have more staff and more beds.
Help to encourage people to put litter in the bin
Or rubbish that is lying on the ground
To pick it up and bin it.

Brendan Dunn (9)

If I Were Prime Minister

If I were Prime Minister
I would have unhealthy food every meal,
If I were Prime Minister
I would make a medicine to make all cuts heal.

If I were Prime Minister
I would raise pocket money to fifty pounds,
If I were Prime Minister
I wouldn't have dog pounds.

If I were Prime Minister
I would abolish homework forever,
If I were Prime Minister
We would all live happily together.

If I were Prime Minister
This country wouldn't go to war,
If I were Prime Minister
I would have carpet on every floor.

If I were Prime Minister . . .

Emily Conway (11)

My Rules

If I were Prime Minister
I would be very sinister
I would ban homework
Make school fun
Be allowed to take chocolate in
Have a sticky bun
Not wear school uniform
Wear your own clothes
Send all the teachers home
Put nail varnish on your toes
Be allowed to eat in fancy restaurants
Every single day
Never have to do chores
Just have fun and play
Have £100 pocket money
Spend it all on toys
Be allowed to put the music on
And make a lot of noise!

Sophie Moss (9)

If Kids Ruled . . .

We would make chocolate a healthy food,
Adults never get in a bad mood,
All children's things will be free,
Adults have to pay loads just for tea!

Children are always allowed on the internet,
If we are good, we can have a free pet,
Adults can never, ever get drunk,
We'll get rid of every punk.

England aren't allowed to start a war,
We will make more money and give it to the poor,
Everyone will start to feed,
All those people that are in need.

Everybody has a real tan,
Children can drive a real van,
Everyone has things that are cool,
Adults think that kids rule!

Rosie Whitaker (10)

If I Were Prime Minister . . .

If I were Prime Minister
I wouldn't be sinister,
Like George Bush or Tony Blair,
I'd be good and kind and very fair . . .

Harry Hill as Minister of Fun,
Oh yes, he's the one,
As Minister of Literature, Brian Jacques,
He'd fill us in with the 'Redwall' facts.

Steve Jackson as Minister of Game,
With his multiple claims to fame.
I'd give the troublemakers lots to do,
Then they'd be too busy to bother people like me and you.

I'd do some things about global warming,
I've also got other ideas forming.
By the time I'm done,
This country will be much more fun!

Robert Winslade (10)

The Country In My Control

With the country in my control,
People will have a better soul,
The number of people with smiley faces
Will be a whole, not a fraction,
Cos of all the cool stuff that will be put in action . . .

People will call me Master G
And troublemakers will be scared when they deal with me!

Children will have zombie dinosaurs for pets
And if parents disagree, they'll pay me big debts!

Poor people will all be sent into a big house,
They will be treated with care and never see a mouse!

Houses will be made out of candy
And there will be a singing stadium
Judged my American Idol Judge Randy!

There'll be tiny robots going into your brain,
Helping crazy people not to go insane!

To stop polluting the air, instead of oil,
Everybody will have hamster-powered cars
And these extra speedy hamsters
Will be kept in metal jars.

My final mission will be to give everyone the ability to fly
And make foxes breakdance . . . don't really know why!

And remember
Kids rule
And adults drool!

Gilead Narh (10)

Cool Rules

Would you ground your parents,
Or go to your Xbox and play?
You could do anything you want,
If you were Prime Minister for the day!

You could get portraits of anything,
Or force a choir from school to sing.
You could even buy a diamond ring
And maybe be as rich as the king.

Would you make some people serve chocolate and chips,
Or make them build a money machine?
They would have to work very hard,
To get you on the big screen.

Or would you be more friendly
And share money with the poor?
They would be so grateful,
It would be you who they adore!

Shaquille Rayes (9)

Kids Rule!

If I ran the country,
It would be so cool.
We'd have lots of animals
And make the rule.
We'd have everything we ever wanted
And stay up late
And maybe, just maybe, have tea with Catherine Tate.
For brekkie we'd have chocolate,
For lunch we'd have chips.
A kitten called Mitzy
And life would be pips!

Justine & Rachael Keeling (8)

The Country Of Me

I'd give all schools more holidays,
I'd make the bad all change their ways,
I'd listen to what everyone says,
This is the way it would be!

Send packages to those so poor and needy,
Abolish those who are selfish and greedy,
Make sure there's room for talented and speedy,
This is the way it would be!

Listen to all the Eco situations,
Concentrate on new explorations,
Carry out new and exciting investigations,
This is the way it would be!

Do what's best for others and not just for me,
Consider friends' feelings and respect their privacy,
If I were ruler of the country,
This is the way it would be!

Ruth Dempster (10)

Untitled

As Prime Minister, I'm proud to say,
All the rules that are set today.
Now all kids can go to bed late,
No more mums saying, 'In bed by eight!'
No more nasty Brussels sprouts,
Fish 'n' chips are what it's about.
Now instead of silly school
We walk around, chat and be cool.
No more housework, that's for Dad,
Instead, have fun or just play had.
No more homework, not for us,
Why don't you just kick up a fuss?
Instead of school lunch, have KFC,
These rules are cool, they're just like me!

Jazmine James (14)

If Kids Ruled

If kids ruled, they would:

Eat and drink what they like,
Get their parents to buy them a bike,
Get £100 in their allowance every week,
Have parents to serve chocolate ice cream,
Because kids are all on one team,
Have a free, luxury house,
Candy on the cars,
Toffee on the bars,
No chores,
No serious wars,
Have no school,
But a big pool.

If kids ruled
They would have a ball!

Syeda Tahmina Khatun (11)

My Very Own Britain!

My Britain has . . .
Houses made of gold,
My Britain has . . .
Jacuzzis warm and cold!

My Britain has . . .
Money for the poor,
My Britain has . . .
Greenhouses here in store!

My Britain has . . .
Cool cars for you to ride,
My Britain has . . .
Sandy beaches and high tides!

My Britain has . . .
Laptops and PS2s,
My Britain has . . .
Game Boys for you to use!

Schools that are cool,
Where all children rule,
Kindness not blindness
And respect to the highness!

That's *my* Britain!

Qudsiyah-Bano Agha-Shah (9)

Untitled

Free creamy chocolate on Monday
No school on Tuesday
Swimming centre open all day on Wednesday
Fair from 9.00 in the morning
To 9.00 at night on Thursday
No reading, no working on Friday
Saturday is camping night
Sunday is free film day
On the third month of the year
Everyone is invited to watch tons of films
And go to the Bolton Museum
On Valentine's Day all presents are free
Comics and mags are free all year round
On Christmas Day all children are allowed
To go to the shops and buy whatever they want
Teachers are sacked if they shout at you once.
Choose me for PM!

Leila Safi (9)

Peace Not War

For every person born,
How many lives are lost?
Although they fight for peace,
Is it worth the cost?
So, if I ruled the world,
And could make any single law,
For the sake of all the families,
I know I would ban war.

Talk instead of fighting,
Words instead of brawls,
Think instead of rushing,
Wise men instead of fools.
Smiles instead of bullet wounds,
Love instead of hate,
Everyone's decision counts,
Deciding our own fate.

Would we make new friends,
Out of those who were our foe?
Would we learn to share and give,
Say yes instead of no?
Nobody is perfect,
But our faults are not a crime,
If we love both the good and bad,
We'll understand in time.

Mothers, fathers, daughters, sons,
All deserve a life.
Someone to be there for you,
Serenity, not strife.
Think of all the life they'd be,
How many people saved.
But we can only start afresh,
Once we regret how we behaved.

So, if I ruled the world
And could make any single law.
For the sake of all I know and love,
I know I would ban war.

Hollie Johnson (15)

Kids Rule

My dad he went to Iraq,
He was lucky, he came back,
Other soldiers do not get that chance,
To come home alive and dance,
I would send all the soldiers home
And knight them for bravery in the Millennium Dome.

I believe everyone should have a house,
That is not infested with woodlouse,
They will all be heated and stocked up with food,
To create a welcoming mood,
All will have water, hot and cold
And will contain furniture, new and old.

Each week school classes must have two lessons of PE,
It will improve the children's health, you see!
One must be outdoors, in the playground or on the grass,
The other should be inside, but of course, both *must* contain
All of your class,
If this does not happen in your school,
All you have to do is make a few calls.

Why do people commit crimes for drugs?
I would sort out these nasty bugs,
Safer streets are what we need,
It would be nice if they were clean,
Murder is a thing that *must not* be done,
Let's all get on and have some fun.

Let us hear the dentist say,
'No, you do not have to pay,'
Let us hear the doctors speak,
'We'll take you straight through, you look bleak,'
No more bills, for your filling,
No more queues, for the living.

Sweets for every single meal,
Not one bone in our body will we have to heal,

Over pocket money, parents will have no control,
We'll take the money down the street
And see the police on patrol,
Down the park we will go, any day that we please
And meet all our friends with dirty knees.

Laura Rochford (11)

Kids Rule

If I were Prime Minister there would be . . .

Chicken and chips,
Untidy rooms,
Tons of chocolate,
Kids rule!

Lots of pocket money,
Gravy with every meal,
Late nights,
Kids rule!

Chill out days,
Every day,
TV blasting,
Kids rule!

No homework,
Music loud,
No parents,
Kids rule!

If I ran the country,
Britain would be heaven,
With no demanding parents,
Kids would rule!

Chloe Trevelyan (13)

Kids Rule

If I ran the country
Rainforests would be in your way
Power stations would be gone
And it'd be sunny every day.

If I ran the country
Sweets would be fruit and veg
Chocolates would be healthy
And adults would be on the edge.

If I ran the country
There'd be no such things as brothers
No schools, no rules, no teachers
And everyone friends with each other.

If I ran the country
I'd be worshipped like a queen
No washing up, no chores to do
And everyone would stay teens.

If only I ruled the country!

Rebecca Davies (13)

Kids Rule!

If I were Prime Minister
I would . . .
Make parents pay
Taxes for children
No uniform at school
Kids rules, yes they do!

If parents didn't obey,
What all the children say
They would get locked up
With a ferocious pup
Kids rule, yes they do!

Kids could have parties
And eat tonnes of Smarties
Chocolates for tea
All for me!

To be cool
Kids have to rule
Kids rule
Yes they do!

Mariam Ayatollahzadeh (12)

Kids Rule

If kids ruled the world
I would change veggies into money
If kids ruled the world
It would always be sunny
If kids ruled the world
I'd eat sweets till I'm sick
If kids ruled the world
I'd have a remote like on 'Click'
If kids ruled the world
I would have no school
If kids ruled the world
I'd turn it into a giant pool
If kids ruled the world
I'd have everything I want
If kids ruled the world
I'd have everything!

Martin Teale (12)

Kids Rule

If I were the prime minister,
I'd be a millionaire,
I could do whatever I want
Whenever I want
And nobody would even care
Because I would be the leader
No one else but me
The country would be a dream world
For everyone to see.

If I were the prime minister
There would be no parents moaning
No homework
No teachers
Telling me what to do
Because I would be the leader
No one else, but me
The country would be a dream world
For everyone to see.

Alice Carrington (12)

Kids Rule

Kids rule
No one likes school
So, if I were Prime Minister
School would be cool.

Pocket money rates would be sky-high
Every day of the week, we'd have cherry pie
And no one would ever
Have to wear a tie.

There would not be a bedtime
Man, this is getting harder to rhyme
Also, the water
Would taste of lemon and lime.

William Binzi (12)

Kids Rule

If I were Prime Minister
I would fly to poor countries
And feed them all some food
As they would be hungry

I would save the dying
And stop child abuse
I would change the sky to green
Make birds fly backwards
Shops that were free!

Making people happy all around the world
Millionaires are common
Poor people are rare
Smiling faces, smiles all around
Schools burn down
All of them!

Sun never goes in
Pets that can talk
Money, money, money
Kids neglect the needles
And going to the hospital
Smoking banned for life.

Houses made from chocolate
Chocolate for breakfast
And for dinner
And for lunch
And for supper.

Bethany Radford (12)

Kids Rule!

Kids rule
Adults drool,
Ruling is cool
'Cause there would be no school.
There would be no five a day
Because all we would do
Is play and play.
No silly homework
For us to do.
By the way
This poem includes
You too!

Ella Taylor (10)

Kids Rule

To run this country my way,
Everyone must be happy every day.

Pollution will no longer fill our air,
You will have to recycle with thoughtfulness and care.

Religion will be a thing of the past,
We will all be equal and no one last.

For crime you will be punished, none will beat the law,
Everyone must work and no one will be poor.

We will have no littering, we will have to use a bin,
Be kind to animals and let nature win.

We should appreciate what we've got,
The people in Africa are dying because it's too hot.

Our country will be good, if we treat it with respect,
So live by my rules and there will be no regret.

Sophia Seminerio (9)

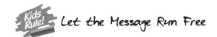

Kids Rule

If I could rule the country
The word 'chores' would be eliminated!

Nobody would have
To look sophisticated!

Homework would be abolished
School would only be about fun.

If I ruled the country for five minutes
I'd have grown-ups on the run!

Sophia Martin (10)

If I Were The Prime Minister

P eople would care about the environment
R uling England
I would change the country
M aking the streets safer at night
E ating at least two vegetables or fruit a day

M aking the councils care about the towns
I would say that every child would not have to do their chores
N ever again will kids have tests or homework
I would make life so much better and easier
S isters would not fight
T eachers, no such thing
E rasers that could rub out people's minds of school
R uler forever, I'd have medals from the Queen.

Rebecca Blair (9)

Kidz Rool!

If kids could rule
I would show you
That we could do
What we want to do.
School would be two hours long
We'd get away with everything wrong
Pocket money would be ten pounds a day
And we would always get our own way.
Toy shops would be free
Because kids rule, you see!
Chocolate would be good for us
Limos would come instead of the bus
We would stay up late watching TV
And sleep in till it was time for tea!
It would be so cool
If kids could rule!

Heleana Neil (10)

If This Year

If this year the country sees
An alternative prime minister,
Then I would like him to be
Great and not so sinister.

A ruler who's among the best
And lives up to his word
And not a man whom I detest
And tells us things absurd.

One who can end the war in Iraq
And bring our troops back home
And one who gives kids things they lack
So we do not feel alone.

All in all, I want this year
A leader with a brain
A leader whom we like to hear
And doesn't go insane.

Rhys Owens (14)

Kidz Rule

These are the rules you must change
Which everybody must obey
No homework must be done
Actually, no school will be fun
But if you want to go to school
You're allowed to go once a month.

No consequences for people
Being such a fool
Though robbers and murderers
Should go to jail.

Pocket money must be increased
You must agree
You can't get grounded
Because we've got a right to be free
Shopping spree in the city
No money has to be paid.

I hope this will come true one day
If a miracle happens again.

Moeko Takane (11)

If I Were To Rule The Country

If I were to rule the country
Me and no one else
People would not be cruel
Everybody would be happy
Even me, myself.

Everybody would have nice houses
With nice and pleasant food
People would have nice clothes
And never be in the nude.

Everyone in this country
That makes it not a nice place
I would have them exiled
And they will be put in disgrace.

What a nice place!

Naomi Spencer (11)

The Prime Minister

If I became prime minister
I would change the way we live,
We would all have happier faces,
Go to lots of fun places,
Be kind to each other,
Always love one another,
The rich would be poorer, so everyone was equal,
Children could eat chocolate, crisps and sweets,
All my favourite treats,
Adults would slow down, having more time to chat,
No scary wars or weapons,
Don't even think of that!

If I became prime minister
Children would have the right to vote,
Banish this 'n' that,
The environment would be safe,
I would ban 4x4s and cigarettes,
Penguins, polar bears and seals would still have ice,
Children would never catch lice,
I would grow lots of trees
Still bounce on Granny's knees,
At last, homework would be a thing of the past,
Quick, quick, please, vote me, Chloe,
I would do all this
If I became prime minister.

Chloe Rushbrooke (10)

Kids Rule!

Us kids rule
From now on
Nothing will stop us
Until we get what we want!

Parents shall serve us pizza and chips
At every meal
And
Should give us everything we want
And let us make a deal.

Us kids rule
From now on
Nothing will stop us
Until we get what we want!

Brothers and sisters
Shall respect us like a queen
And
Share all their toys with us
And not be so mean.

Us kids rule
From now on
Nothing will stop us
Until we get what we want!

Neighbours shall allow us to play music
From dusk till dawn
And
Let us run free
In the fields of corn.

Us kids rule
From now on
Nothing will stop us
Until we get what we want!

Teachers shall be less strict
And be forbidden to tell us what to do
And
Shall be able to have fun
Just like me and you.

Leah Jakeman (11)

Untitled

If I were to rule the country
I would knock down houses to build trees
I would make the ice caps freeze
I'd turn a book into lots of money
And I'd make the clouds a bit sunny
I'd make a horrible mummy's curse
Into a lovely chocolate purse
And I would make the most boring book
Into a very skilled chocolate cook.

Eden Allen (7)

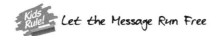

Everybody Be A Friend

Everybody be a friend
The thing is, it's supposed to never end
Everyone listen at school
Don't act like a fool
All good people should be free
Everybody should be happy with glee
That's the kids' rules.

Emma Jane Hesketh (8)

Kids Rule

If I were Prime Minister
I would make,
The rule that all the kids
Should not go to school
And I'd say what would be funny
I would make all the banks
Give me all their money
I would go to the supermarket
And fill up my trolley
With lots of sweets
That would be jolly
Then I would go home and tell my mum and dad
Exactly what time I was going to bed!

Jamie Fraser

Kids Rule

Start all school days at seven
And finish at eleven
Have a swimming pool
To relax and be cool.

Don't worry about being late
When you walk into school with your mate
No need to worry
When your parents hand out lots of pocket money.

So, if I were Prime Minister
And was making the rules
I would put into force
The last four rules
By making sure people turn off their lights
When not in use late at night.

Callum Chadwick (9)

Kids Rule

Parents can go to school instead of kids
And be served only hot dinners
With chicken, peas, potatoes, sprouts
Lettuce, broccoli, sweetcorn and carrots
Every day
Give them six pieces of homework
And give them fifty pence on Fridays
Plus on Christmas, a special treat of chips
Cakes and one chocolate bar
And fish with beans
The bullies would be sent to the school dungeon
The teachers would be kids
And wouldn't get a day off
Except for Christmas and the summer holidays
And the head teacher would be me.

Holly Davies (8)

Kids Rule!

If I were Prime Minister, you would see
The biggest change that there could be
All schools would be taught for an hour a day
And the rest of the time, the children could play
We would serve the teachers a Jamie Oliver meal
And the kids could eat whatever they feel.

Give teachers homework, they can't make a mistake
If they do, they will miss their break
At home time the kids must be taken to the shop
To buy lots of sweets, crisps and pop
At bedtime parents go to bed at eight
And all children get to stay up *late!*

Katie Edwardson (8)

Kids Rule

To be prime minister, I know I should
Make it a world where everything's good
But I'm tempted to make it compulsory
To ban homework and broccoli
I'd have ice cream and chocolate for breakfast and tea
And all the children could come and join me
To have a discussion on world poverty
My brother and sister could not boss me
I would be the head of my family
I would watch TV in my room all day
Then solve everyone's problems and go out to play!

Billy Burke (9)

Kids Rule!

If I were Prime Minister
I would make all adults and parents go to school
I would make them be my servants
And what I say they would do
Even when they just come in from school.
I would go shopping and get everything for free
I would change the uniform so they could wear what they want.
If I were Prime Minister, I would put the school years to Year 20
They would have homework every day
And make the years harder, even reception class.
I would get money every day
And I would give some to the poor
And make the cars a lot better
I would make sure everybody was happy
And everything was in good condition
If only I were Prime Minister.

Thomas Hughes (9)

Kids Rule!

If I were Prime Minister
I would ban sprouts, tomatoes
And carrots too
So watch out you teachers
I might ban you!

School would become a 4-day week
Making children go five days a week is such a cheek.

So, no more homework of English or maths
I would spend my time at the swimming baths.

I'd make Toys 'R' Us very cheap
Children's pocket money would be £20 a week.

So, hopefully you'll vote for me
I am the best
Much better than all the rest!

Lucy Dunne (8)

Kids Rule!

If I ruled, I wouldn't let kids eat fruit or veg
If I ruled, I would let kids stay up late
If I ruled, I would make grown-ups do what the kids want
If I ruled, I would make grown-ups do all the work
And go to school.

Kayleigh Ann Ineson (8)

Kids Rule!

If I were Prime Minister
I would be so cool
I'd make all the parents go to school
I would give the poor some more money
I would hire a servant and a cook
I would pay them one penny a month
I would stop all the bullying and make bullies nice
All my changes would come at a price
I would stop all the fighting in the world
That's what I would do!

Elisabeth Bowskill (8)

Kids Rule!

If I were Prime Minister, I'd do what I could,
I'd make sure that people did not fight,
If I ruled the country, I'd make it better,
I would make sure the poor had more,
If I were Prime Minister, I wouldn't like people to be sad,
I'd try to stop bullying and all things bad,
If I ruled the country, I don't think it's likely,
But blimey, if I did, it would be quite exciting!

Mica Woods (8)

Kids Rule!

If I were in charge for a day
Everything would be my way
I would demolish school
I really am no fool
There would be no teacher's pets
But the teachers would be my pets
They would drink from an old dog's bowl
Spend the rest of the day in a hole
We'd leave them there for the day
So we could get on with our play
We'd cover the teachers in gunk
And get on with eating our junk
No fruit and veg for me
You can chuck it in the sea
If I were in charge, you'd see
This is how it would be.

Oliver Gill

Kids Rule!

If I were Prime Minister
I would make parents go to school and do homework
If I were Prime Minister
I would make chocolate and smoothies my school dinners
If I were Prime Minister
I would make everyone be kind to each other at all times
If I were Prime Minister
I would make people protect their environment forever
If I were Prime Minister
I would make the rich give money to the poor
If I were Prime Minister
I would make everyone go to school, except children.

Wendy Anne Hart (9)

Kids Rule!

If I were the minister of prime
Then every day would be fun time
We'd get up late in the morning
This would stop us from yawning
Adults would have to give us money
For breakfast, it's pancakes covered in honey
Now we go to school for our mark
The rest of the day in the park
Then it's time for a meal
I'll have what I feel
Back to our fun and game
That is our only aim
It's chocolate and chips for tea
It's the only thing for me
Now it's time for TV
My life is just so easy
I'll fall asleep in my bed
Not a care in my head.

Joshua Gill (8)

Untitled

When I get older, I will be,
The person who rules our country
And this is how I dream it will be,
Fighting, shouting and wars will end,
Everyone will be nice and kind and be your friend,
Schools as good as ours should be everywhere,
No more teachers who just don't care,
Children will learn to share and care,
We will make the environment clean,
Picking up litter and no more fumes, this will mean,
More big parks with slides and swings,
No more staying in on computers and things,
Schools will have healthy foods,
This will help everyone to work and get rid of nasty moods,
The prime minister can eat chocolate and sweets,
With all this hard work, I will need some treats,
All of my plans, I am sure will work,
So vote for Prime Minister . . .

Chloe McQuirk!

Chloe McQuirk (9)

Kids Rule!

Kids would have sweets for every meal,
Parents would do your homework,
You get a rocket when you are five,
You leave school when you are six,
You have to be five to drink,
Every day is Christmas Day,
No schoolwork ever,
Ban fruit,
McDonald's for school dinners,
Abolish poverty,
No water allowed,
Free ice cream for all!

Sam Underhill (8)

Kids Rule

If I were Prime Minister
I would tell the children
That they could tell the adults what to do,
Oh yes, what I am writing is all going to be true!
I would tell the rich to pay the poor,
So then I don't think the poor will go hungry anymore.
I would like everyone to have a good time
And that is why I am writing this rhyme.
I would tell people to share,
As well, I would tell people to care.
I would ask the children to say to their parents
That they want chocolate and bubblegum for every meal.
I would say to the children, do not steal.
I would make adults pay a huge amount of money,
Even if they just want to buy some honey.
I am glad you have given up your time,
Just to read this rhyme.
Remember, kids rule!
And if I were Prime Minister
I would make all adults go to school!

Jordan Preston (8)

Untitled

If I were Prime Minister
Then I would;
Say that school was only on Mondays
And there would be a cinema and a bowling alley
In every town and city
There would be no uniforms
And everything in Blackpool would be £4 or less
Every child must have a horse and stables
And their bedrooms should be decorated as they wish
All the soldiers must come back from Iraq
And there should be more money given to Africa.

Charlotte Hughes (8)

Untitled

If I were Prime Minister for just one day,
I'd help the world in every possible way.
All the children would be smiling,
Everyone would be having fun.
I'd do my best to stop the rain
And bring out the shining sun.
I'd share out all the money,
With everyone who's poor.
No one would go to bed hungry
And peace would take over the war.

Joe Lyons (9)

Kids Rule!

If I were Prime Minister, I'd . . .

Stop cruelty to animals and children,
Make sure every shop closed at 10pm on a Sunday,
Stop people littering,
Make every child tell their parents what to do,
Let people have a say in what's going on in England.

Erin Cluskey (8)

Kids Rule!

Tony Blair is retiring this year,
Let's bring out a big cheer.
If I was the prime minister,
It would be a nicer place to be,
A nicer place to be,
If the prime minister were me.
All the soldiers would come home,
Then they wouldn't have to moan.
Less time at school so children could play,
Then they would have much more to say.
Five a day would be banned and junk food would rule,
Now that is cool!
Parents would have more time with their kids,
Visiting places we never knew existed.
Thank goodness it's not like this,
Or we wouldn't see our teacher, who we call Miss!

Matthew Mahoney (9)

Kids Rule!

If I could rule the country,
I'd make people give money to charity.
I wouldn't let maths take part in school,
Now that would be really cool.
All the schools would be knocked down,
Even if people laughed or frowned.
I would only let shops serve chips and sweets,
Most of all, I'd ban red meat.
I'd ban being grounded or any punishment,
Everyone would go camping in a tent.
People who commit crimes would pay,
They would stay in prison every day.
I would give everyone a garden, house and pool,
If only, if only, if only, I ruled the country and schools!

Georgia Williams (9)

Untitled

If I were Prime Minister, I would say,
That all the old teachers should go away.
I'd make it so that children would rule the school,
Now that's a thought, that's really cool.
It would be fun to have ICT all day,
If I were Prime Minister, I would make it that way.
I'd make watching TV a lesson,
I'd also make every boy stop messin'.
I would make girls go to a separate school,
Away from all the boys that smell and drool.
Being Prime Minister would be fun,
But I would never get the job done.

Roisin Fletcher (8)

Untitled

If I lived at Number 10,
I would make it into the coolest den.
Homework would be scrapped
And replaced with PlayStations and Xboxes.
Adult programmes would stop at 3.10pm
Only things children want to watch.
Remotes out of bounds for parents,
I would declare world peace with chocolate and sweets,
Eat ice cream and chips on the same plate,
Kids would decide how much pocket money
They would get every day,
Free holidays for all OAPs,
Especially those with knobbly knees!

George Edwards (8)

If I Were . . .

If I were to run the country,
There would be no killing,
Nor would there be murders or deaths,
No one would have allergies or diseases,
Every child will have pocket money,
All things in the world would be furry.

Kerri Ogg (11)

Untitled

If I were Prime Minister
I would ban smoking
To stop people from choking
And I'd ban all schools
But instead, go to the pool
I'd like everyone to stay at the park
Because we would have a lark
And I'd like to save all animals
By stopping all the hunting.

Lauren Gallie (9)

If I Were Prime Minister

If I were Prime Minister
What would I do?
Lessen global warming
That's what I'd do.

If I were Prime Minister
What would I do?
Try to stop poverty
That's what I'd do.

If I were Prime Minister
What would I do?
I'd help pensioners
That's what I'd do.

If I were Prime Minister
What would I do?
If I were Prime Minister
I would help you.

Jill Marshall (11)

Kids Rule

Us kids rule
It's a pity we didn't make the rules up
Why if I did
I would make adults do children's chores
And ban tobacco
The world would live in peace
Every child would have a friend
We would have a healthy diet
We would be clever
My dreams might come true
But the alien adults won't let us.

Alyx Harrison (10)

If I Were To Lead Britain

I would take away all the pain
So it didn't leave a stain.

I would save the polar ice caps
And the little polar bears
To save their pretty habitats
To show that we care.

I would stop poverty
To feed the young children
Under their payment
Of death and destruction.

Hannah Smith (11)

Untitled

I would make people share their money
With the poor and lonely,
All the nasty things like drugs
Got rid of, as well as the thugs,
The children would be happy and carefree
Without any homework and playing with glee,
The injured wild animals would be cared for too
In their own surroundings, not in a zoo,
Our environment would be clean and green
The waste is nowhere to be seen,
We'll stage the Olympic Games, weather not too cold,
With Great Britain going for gold.

Sarah Hancock (11)

If I Were . . .

If I were the ruler and led the way
We would not have to go to school every day
Instead, we'd run and jump and play
And skip around the house all day.

I'd make sure we had no chores to do
Because we'd rather go to the zoo.

I'd pass a rule that would say
We didn't have to eat stew or celery
Instead, we would eat chocolate
And all of those tasty treats.

I'd make sure poor people
Did not live on the streets
And had plenty of money
And food to eat.

That is what I think I would do
If I were the one
Who made all the rules.

Sally Bruce (10)

If I Were Prime Minister

I would make our country better,
I would make it a fun place,
I would give everyone ice cream,
So I could see a smile upon their face.

Bradley Bishop (9)

If I Were Prime Minister

If I were Prime Minister
There would be less school
We'd do maths, English, RE
And for break will play ball.

If I were Prime Minister
Kids would be kind
They'd clean up once a week
And help birds with poor beaks.

If I were Prime Minister
Meals of the day would be great
Chocolate and sweets all day long
And veggies a day, around eight.

If I were Prime Minister
People would be funny
Comedy acts plus loads more things
Don't forget rappers in cool bling.

If I were Prime Minister
I'd turn England pink
We'd call boy dogs Zonk and Zank
And girl dogs would be called Zunk and Zink.

Well, this is my idea
Of me as Prime Minister
You probably think it's weird
What would you do if you were Prime Minister?
Would everyone have curly beards?

Lara Keene (10)

Kids Rule

If I were President
I would make the country
Not have riots, wars, bullying or racism
If I were President
All poor people
Would be able to have a home
In a special care place
Until they earned a bit of money
And could have a better life
That's how kids rule!

Luke Lewis (9)

The Best Job For Me

Prime minister's the job for me
Kind and fair I would be . . .

Towns always clean and smart
For kids to play and have a laugh!

All the toys you could ever need
Nintendos, laptops and PS3s.

All children would get 20 pounds each week
From their parents, to spend or keep!

Taxes and bills would be no more
We would all be wealthy, never poor.

Please vote me Prime Minister!

Harry Lewis (9)

I Have The Power

I'm the prime minister of the UK,
But I'm only ten years old!
It's hard to fit in at school,
Since I'm always the most bold!
I have all the power,
But what good is that
When I have to do what I'm told?
Forgetting Mum, forgetting Dad,
To make the world a better place for *kids!*
I could give every child a phone,
It's as easy as giving a dog a bone!
I would put a roof on every house,
Money by the doorstep,
But that's only the beginning,
Cos no one tells me what to do!
School would start at 12.00 and finish at 2.00pm
Make weekends three days long,
In my world, things can never go wrong!
Cos no one tells me what to do!
So much to do, so little time,
So just for the grown-ups,
We will eat vegetables,
Candy veggies that is!
If only all of that were true,
I lied from the beginning!
Imagine if kids ruled the world,
But that was only a daydream.

Georgina Morris (10)

Untitled

I am Prime Minister, so do what I say,
Otherwise, you will pay!
Say bye, bye to school,
Kids will always swim in the pool.
Parents, you are our cleaners,
I'm just getting meaner and meaner.
Midnight feasts until we pop,
I will never, ever stop
Just give me more money,
This is getting better than honey!
Have a party every day
I'll be writing this until May!
Let me sleep in until lunch:
And then I'll have a little munch!
Get a chocolate fountain for my room,
It better be in there very soon
Make a dungeon for the bad,
You may think I'm extremely mad!
Give free chocolate to all kids,
Make sure they're in pots with lids!
Kids will rule the universe
If you disobey me what to do!
Unless you want to live on the moon
They are the laws so follow them
Or else I'll shove you in a den . . .

Amelia Sacks (10)

If I Were Prime Minister

If I were Prime Minister
The show 'Who Wants To Be A Millionaire'
Would be on TV even more
And all the money would go to charity
So someone in Africa would be a billionaire
So they would build hospitals there.

If I were Prime Minister
I would have school lunches every day in every school
And all the lunches are free
There will be more time in school, but less homework
The teachers would make the lessons more fun
The break time would be longer
But the lessons would include a lot of education.

If I were Prime Minister
There would be more bins
So there would be no litter on the floor
In every shop there would be Fair Trade
More hospitals around the world.

Noa Filasof (9)

If I Were . . .

If I were Prime Minister for a week, I would . . .
On Mondays, give food to the poor
On Tuesdays, kids eat only chocolate
On Wednesdays, recycle cardboard
On Thursdays, give all children a holiday
On Fridays, give to charity
On Saturdays, ban homework
On Sundays, save the planet.
What a busy week!

Jonah Zur (7)

Kidz Rule

If I were in charge of the country
I'd serve chocolate every day
There would be discos every night
Lovely lemonade
Icy ice cream
Chocolate coins for money
Skateboards for transportation
SpongeBob Squarepants TV shows
Wings for flight
Rocket shoes for speed.

Michael Harrison (9)

Kids Rule

If I were in charge of the country,
I'd serve fish and chips every day.
If I were in charge of the country,
The kids would all shout, *'Hooray!'*
If I were in charge of the country,
Ice creams and cakes would be free.
If I were in charge of the country,
The kids would all get a key.

If I were really the king,
Money would be the thing.
If I were really the king,
No one would have to sing.
If I were really the king,
School would be shut down today.
If I were really the king,
Clubs would be on every day.

Kids rule!

Ben Owen (9)

Kids Rule!

If I were in charge of the country
I'd serve chips every day
I would make a chocolate mountain
And make it explode in May.

Poor people would not exist
Everyone would have millions
I would rule in a castle
And I would have billions.

I would be king
I'd rule the United States
And when I have pizza
I'd clear my plate.

If I were King
Because kids should rule the world!

Sebastian Herdman (9)

My Zone

If I were in charge of the country
I'd make a few simple rules:
Like no one be disgusting
And no one *ever* drool
Cigarettes I would make a class A drug
All toddlers have teddies for bedtime hugs
I'd make all of England a land of justice and peace
And at the sound of my voice, evil would tremble and cease
Everyone would have zero maths lessons a week
But I've still to come to the spectacular peak . . .
Everything is free!
But . . .
But don't be greedy!

Matthew Fairhurst (9)

If I Were In Charge Of The Country

If I were in charge of the country,
I'd make everyone give £2 to the poor,
Or maybe even more!
I'd stop global warming from killing polar bears,
I'd make a shop selling lots and lots of pears,
I'd make every Friday apple day
And nobody would pay,
I'd give homeless people homes,
I'd have a lot of garden gnomes!
I'd change my name to Beenie
And watch Fizz the Tweenie!

Raephena Ruhl-Young (9)

Kids Rule!

K   ids have chocolate every day
I   ce cream for free
D   iscos every night
S   pongeBob Squarepants TV shows

R   eligious Education never again
U   kuleles playing
L   ovely lemonade
E   verybody to be nice.

James Askew (8)

Kids Rule!

P oor people rich
R ide on horses with flowers and hearts for the paths
I cing cakes then eating them
M idnight Mass at Christmastime
E veryone is nice to everyone

M ake cookies and cakes with chocolate flakes
I ce skating every Monday
N ice knitting for grannies, not for kids
I cing sour cakes
S chool, but *no* homework
T asting competitions every weekend
E at sandwiches every day
R ide motorbikes for fun, but don't get hurt.

Kezia Clark (10)

Kids Rule!

If I were the prime minister,
I would not be sinister,
I would make Britain a happy place,
You would see a smile on everybody's face,
I would make the people pay,
So kids in poor countries can play,
If I were the prime minister
Nobody would be sinister
I would make everybody healthy
And I would make the poor wealthy
What would you do if you were the PM?
Hopefully nothing bad,
Whenever I say
Kids will be free to play
If I were the *prime minister*.

Daniel Kirkpatrick (11)

Kids Rule

If I were in charge,
No one would barge,
Past me when I'm shopping,
Chips would be healthy
And kids would be wealthy,
If I were in charge.
Every day I'd go downtown
And wear a silver crown,
Poor would get money
And bees make more honey
If I were in charge.
I'd have gardens of roses
And soft, little toses
If I was in charge
Yes, if I had power
I would be as nice as a golden flower.

Emily Watt (10)

Kids Rule!

P ray for sick people
R aise money for poor and sick people
I would help others
M ake poverty history
E ncourage people to give money

M ake schools healthy
I would help stop climate change
N ever hurt someone's feelings
I would always care for others
S ave the environment
T each others that don't have money
E xplain why we should help
R ecycle as much as you can.

Rachel Knox (10)

My Laws

If I were to change the laws,
I'd ban all brothers' mucky paws,
I'd make teachers do all kids' homework,
They can't refuse, they cannot smirk,
I'd stop world wars, it's about others too,
I'd give people in poverty a flushing loo!
Fair Trade is important, I find it grand,
All clothing must have a Fair Trade brand,
No bullies, no fights, no slaughter, that's bad
It makes the families, oh so sad,
Stop being so bad, it's oh, such a pest,
Living in my world would be the best.

Raine Alexandra Gladdy (11)

Freedom

P ocket money every day
R eading will always exist, read every day
I will make sure everyone supports a team in football
M aths will be P1, maths all the time
E veryone has to be fair, including the prime minister

M onkeys as pets
I wish I could be Prime Minister
N obody is left out
I would shout out, 'Kids rule!'
S chools get blown up
T eachers never exist
E ndangered species always helped
R obots are invented.

David McLennan Stephen (10)

If I Were . . .

If I were Prime Minister
I would make
Parents pay kids
I would tell teachers
You're not getting paid
I would let kids
Eat all they wanted
Only kids would get paid
Let kids do what they want
Let every kid get a free plasma TV
And go to a theme park
And get in free.

Tara Cameron (10)

Kids Rule!

When I rule the country
I'll be as happy as I can be
When I rule the country
Everyone will look up at me.

Rule number one
Is teachers must be nice
And if they aren't
They'll have to pay the price.

Rule number two
Is the best by far
Everyone must drive
In a snazzy car.

My third rule
Number three
Everyone must
Respect me.

My fourth rule
Comes with a bash
Parents must pay kids
Loads of cash.

Rule number five
Is last but not least
The whole world
Should be at peace.

When I rule the country
I'll be as happy as can be
When I rule the country
Everyone will look up at me.

Rhiannon Widger (10)

Untitled

It would be so cool
If kids could rule
No homework and no school
I would make all the adults treat us like royalty
And we would always eat candy for our tea
I would eat crisps and sweets all day long
But just doing that feels a bit too wrong
Everyone would recycle and make that the law
So we could help the environment
A little bit more!

Jemima Aspinall (10)

When I Am Prime Minister

When I am Prime Minister
The kids teach the teachers
How to have fun!

The lessons are funny
Lesson one, how to play with chewing gum
Put it in your mouth, then make a balloon
Chewing and chewing your gum!

Lesson two, how to make a mess in the kitchen
First put the flour on the ground
Second put the water in it
Third put your shoes on and start to mix it up
You will have fun.

When I am Prime Minister
The school will be fun
Kids play with the teachers at games
And they win all the time.

But I am not the prime minister
And the school is not fun
The teachers are teaching
And kids do not smile
I sit in the classroom
And think about how it would be
If I were Prime Minister . . .

Zuzanna Marska (10)

Kids Rule

If I were Prime Minister
I would ban homework
I would make adults pay
Pocket money at £5 a week
Then the children would be rich
I would do their trade
I would give money to the poor
I would make adults get us chips and crisps
At school we could throw snowballs.

Callum Stewart (10)

Kids Rule

If I was the head of the country, the PM,
I would make sure that there would be
No homework at all.

Plus England, Scotland,
Northern Ireland and Wales,
Would be a happy place,
A very, very, very happy place.

We wouldn't cut down trees
To our hearts' content
We would save our countries' own wildlife
Stop hunting and save our environment.

Also, we would try to stop
Animals from becoming extinct,
Like the Yangtze river dolphins
Probably are today.

So, if I were PM
We could have a better place
To be and live!

Laura Abbott (10)

Tony Blair

If I were Tony Blair
I'd act like the mayor
I'd be in a dream
I'd make up a new cream
I'd help all the poor
I'd give them a door
Everyone would have millions
But I would have billions
Every person should care
For people who have to share
All of us would love
Every single dove
You wouldn't know who I was
And this is because
Kids should rule!

Lucy Ellerton (9)

Kids Rule!

If I were Prime Minister
I would make swearing the law,
Put all teachers on the sun.
Breaking mirrors brings good luck.
Blow up all schools
And make them into candy shops.
Put cats into space
Instead of dogs and monkeys.

William Moir (10)

Young Writers Information

We hope you have enjoyed reading this book - and that you will continue to enjoy it in the coming years.

If you like reading and writing poetry drop us a line, or give us a call, and we'll send you a free information pack.

Alternatively if you would like to order further copies of this book or any of our other titles, then please give us a call or log onto our website at www.youngwriters.co.uk

Young Writers Information
Remus House
Coltsfoot Drive
Peterborough
PE2 9JX

(01733) 890066

Armistice Day

The war-dead had their solemn pause,
Full uniformed etiquette, mournful sumptuary.
November bugles rouse us living on
who half grudge, half kowtow to this blaze
of rank and gloom, high military trumpery
imposing closure on the dead and gone.

Present, the peace-dead in full fruition
extended into age lives unsacrificed
to state or cause, reserving their consent
and therefore closer to our condition.
Autonomous by choice – that sufficed
to bugle forth these dead as better spent.

Religion

Clergy, ever in grey suits
Atheists in downright black
    contingent agnostics
     ecumenical christians
    in whatever
Damned colour they please.

Immortal Rose

Mortality, according to the rose
was whispered of by one who lied:
as far as any flower knows
no gardener has ever died.

Haiku

formless rags of space
thoughts so limpid – hard to think
they have an author